I0428172

United States Government Accountability Office

GAO

Testimony
Before the Committee on Oversight and
Government Reform, House of
Representatives

For Release on Delivery
Expected at 10:30 a.m. EST
Thursday, February 14, 2013

GAO'S 2013 HIGH-RISK SERIES

An Update

Statement of Gene L. Dodaro
Comptroller General of the United States

Accountability * Integrity * Reliability

GAO-13-359T

HIGH-RISK SERIES

An Update

Highlights of GAO-13-359T, a statement before the Committee on Oversight and Government Reform, House of Representatives

Why GAO Did This Study

The federal government is the world's largest and most complex entity, with about $3.5 trillion in outlays in fiscal year 2012 funding a broad array of programs and operations. GAO maintains a program to focus attention on government operations that it identifies as high risk due to their greater vulnerabilities to fraud, waste, abuse, and mismanagement or the need for transformation to address economy, efficiency, or effectiveness challenges. Since 1990, more than one-third of the areas previously designated as high risk have been removed from the list because sufficient progress was made to address the problems identified.

This biennial update describes the status of high-risk areas listed in 2011 and identifies any new high-risk area needing attention by Congress and the executive branch. Solutions to high-risk problems offer the potential to save billions of dollars, improve service to the public, and strengthen the performance and accountability of the U.S. government.

What GAO Recommends

This report contains GAO's views on progress made and what remains to be done to bring about lasting solutions for each high-risk area. Perseverance by the executive branch in implementing GAO's recommended solutions and continued oversight and action by Congress are essential to achieving progress. GAO is dedicated to continue working with Congress and the executive branch to help ensure additional progress is made.

View GAO-13-359T. For more information, contact J. Christopher Mihm at (202) 512-6806 or mihmj@gao.gov

What GAO Found

In February 2011, GAO detailed 30 high-risk areas. Sufficient progress has been made to remove the high-risk designation from two areas.

- *Management of Interagency Contracting.* Improvements include (1) continued progress made by agencies in addressing identified deficiencies, (2) establishment of additional management controls, (3) creation of a policy framework for establishing new interagency contracts, and (4) steps taken to address the need for better data on these contracts.

- *Internal Revenue Service Business Systems Modernization.* We are removing this area because progress has been made in addressing significant weaknesses in information technology and financial management capabilities. IRS delivered the initial phase of its cornerstone tax processing project and began the daily processing and posting of individual taxpayer accounts in January 2012. This enhanced tax administration and improved service by enabling faster refunds for more taxpayers, allowing more timely account updates, and faster issuance of taxpayer notices. IRS has put in place close to 80 percent of the practices needed for an effective investment management process, including all of the processes needed for effective project oversight.

While these two areas have been removed from the High Risk List, GAO will continue to monitor them.

This year, GAO has added two areas.

- *Limiting the Federal Government's Fiscal Exposure by Better Managing Climate Change Risks.* Climate change creates significant financial risks for the federal government, which owns extensive infrastructure, such as defense installations; insures property through the National Flood Insurance Program; and provides emergency aid in response to natural disasters. The federal government is not well positioned to address the fiscal exposure presented by climate change, and needs a government-wide strategic approach with strong leadership to manage related risks.

- *Mitigating Gaps in Weather Satellite Data.* Potential gaps in environmental satellite data beginning as early as 2014 and lasting as long as 53 months have led to concerns that future weather forecasts and warnings—including warnings of extreme events such as hurricanes, storm surges, and floods—will be less accurate and timely. A number of decisions are needed to ensure contingency and continuity plans can be implemented effectively.

In the past 2 years notable progress has been made in the vast majority of areas that remain on GAO's High Risk List. This progress is due to the combined efforts of the Congress through oversight and legislation, the Office of Management and Budget through its leadership and coordination, and the agencies through their efforts to take corrective actions to address longstanding problems and implement related GAO recommendations.

_____ **United States Government Accountability Office**

GAO's 2013 High Risk List

Strengthening the Foundation for Efficiency and Effectiveness

- Limiting the Federal Government's Fiscal Exposure by Better Managing Climate Change Risks (new)
- Management of Federal Oil and Gas Resources
- Modernizing the U.S. Financial Regulatory System and Federal Role in Housing Finance
- Restructuring the U.S. Postal Service to Achieve Sustainable Financial Viability
- Funding the Nation's Surface Transportation System
- Strategic Human Capital Management
- Managing Federal Real Property

Transforming DOD Program Management

- DOD Approach to Business Transformation
- DOD Business Systems Modernization
- DOD Support Infrastructure Management
- DOD Financial Management
- DOD Supply Chain Management
- DOD Weapon Systems Acquisition

Ensuring Public Safety and Security

- Mitigating Gaps in Weather Satellite Data (new)
- Strengthening Department of Homeland Security Management Functions
- Establishing Effective Mechanisms for Sharing and Managing Terrorism-Related Information to Protect the Homeland
- Protecting the Federal Government's Information Systems and the Nation's Cyber Critical Infrastructures
- Ensuring the Effective Protection of Technologies Critical to U.S. National Security Interests
- Revamping Federal Oversight of Food Safety
- Protecting Public Health through Enhanced Oversight of Medical Products
- Transforming EPA's Processes for Assessing and Controlling Toxic Chemicals

Managing Federal Contracting More Effectively

- DOD Contract Management
- DOE's Contract Management for the National Nuclear Security Administration and Office of Environmental Management
- NASA Acquisition Management

Assessing the Efficiency and Effectiveness of Tax Law Administration

- Enforcement of Tax Laws

Modernizing and Safeguarding Insurance and Benefit Programs

- Improving and Modernizing Federal Disability Programs
- Pension Benefit Guaranty Corporation Insurance Programs
- Medicare Program
- Medicaid Program
- National Flood Insurance Program

Source: GAO.

Mr. Chairman, Ranking Member Cummings, and Members of the Committee:

Thank you for the opportunity to discuss our 2013 high-risk update.[1] Since 1990, GAO has regularly reported on government operations that we have identified as high risk due to their greater vulnerability to fraud, waste, abuse, and mismanagement or the need for transformation to address economy, efficiency, or effectiveness challenges. Our high-risk program, supported by this committee and the Senate Committee on Homeland Security and Governmental Affairs, has brought much-needed focus to problems impeding effective government and costing billions of dollars each year.

Since our last high-risk update in 2011, many notable positive developments have occurred and progress has been made in the vast majority of areas that remain on the list. Congressional oversight and legislative action have been critical to this progress. Congress passed numerous laws—eight of which are discussed in our report—targeting both specific problems and the high-risk areas overall. In addition, top administration officials have continued to show their commitment to ensuring that high-risk areas receive attention and oversight. The Office of Management and Budget (OMB) regularly convenes meetings for agencies to provide progress updates on high-risk issues. When a high-risk issue area ranges across agencies, OMB coordinates with representatives from multiple agencies to participate. These meetings typically include OMB's Deputy Director for Management, participating agencies' representatives to the President's Management Council, other administration and agency staff members responsible for addressing the high-risk issue, as well as myself and others from GAO.

This year, due to significant progress made, we removed the high-risk designation from two areas—Management of Interagency Contracting and the Internal Revenue Service (IRS) Business Systems Modernization. These areas demonstrate how sustained congressional oversight and action, high-level administration attention, efforts of the responsible agencies, and support from GAO through its many

---

[1]GAO, *High-Risk Series: An Update*, GAO-13-283 (Washington, D.C.: February 2013).

recommendations and consistent follow-up on the implementation of recommended actions lead to success in addressing risks.

While there has been notable progress, much remains to be done to address the 30 high-risk issues that are currently on GAO's High Risk List. Our high risk update report and website[2] provide details for each of these issues, describing the nature of the risks, what actions have been taken to address them, and what remains to be done to make further progress. The details in our report, along with successful implementation by agencies and continued oversight by Congress, can form a solid foundation for progress to address risks and improve programs and operations.

This year we designated two new high-risk areas—Limiting the Federal Government's Fiscal Exposure by Better Managing Climate Change Risks and Mitigating Gaps in Weather Satellite Data. Lasting solutions to these and the other 28 high-risk areas offer the potential to save billions of dollars, dramatically improve service to the American public, and strengthen public confidence and trust in the performance and accountability of our national government.

High-Risk Designation Removed

When legislative, administration, and agency actions, including those in response to our recommendations, result in significant progress toward resolving a high-risk problem, we remove the high-risk designation. The five criteria for determining if the high-risk designation can be removed are (1) a demonstrated strong commitment to, and top leadership support for, addressing problems; (2) the capacity to address problems; (3) a corrective action plan; (4) a program to monitor corrective measures; and (5) demonstrated progress in implementing corrective measures.

For our 2013 high-risk update, we determined that the following two areas warranted removal from the High Risk List.

Management of Interagency Contracting

Interagency contracting—where one agency either places an order using another agency's contract or obtains contracting support services from another agency—can help streamline the procurement process, take

---

[2]GAO's high risk website, http://www.gao.gov/highrisk/.

advantage of unique expertise in a particular type of procurement, and achieve savings. While this method of contracting can save the government money and effort when properly managed, it also poses a variety of risks.

In 2005, we designated the management of interagency contracting as high risk due in part to unclear lines of accountability between customer and assisting agencies and the potential for improper use, including out-of-scope work and noncompliance with competition requirements. We identified the continuing need for additional management controls and guidance and clearer definitions of roles and responsibilities as keys to addressing these issues. We have also highlighted challenges agencies faced in fully realizing the benefits of interagency contracts, including the lack of data and the risk of potential duplication when new contracting vehicles are created. To address these issues, we identified the need for a policy framework and business case analysis requirements to support the creation of certain new contracts and improved data on existing interagency contracts.

As detailed in our 2013 high risk update report, we are removing the management of interagency contracting from the High Risk List based on the following:

- *Continued progress in addressing previously identified deficiencies.* In our 2009 and 2011 high-risk updates we noted improvements in procedures used in making purchases on behalf of the Department of Defense (DOD)—the largest user of interagency contracts. The DOD Inspector General has also reported a significant decrease in problems with DOD procurements through other federal agencies in congressionally mandated reviews of interagency acquisitions. More recently, we reported earlier this year that DOD substantially complied with new requirements for interagency contract orders.[3]

- *Strengthened management controls.* In response to congressional direction, Federal Acquisition Regulation (FAR) provisions on interagency acquisitions were revised in 2010 to require that agencies make a best procurement approach determination to justify the use of

---

[3]GAO, *Interagency Contracting: Agency Actions Address Key Management Challenges, but Additional Steps Needed to Ensure Consistent Implementation of Policy Changes,* GAO-13-133R (Washington, D.C.: Jan. 29, 2013).

GAO-13-359T

an interagency contract and prepare written interagency agreements outlining the roles and responsibilities of customer and assisting organizations. OMB's October 2012 analysis of reports from the 24 agencies that account for almost all contract spending governmentwide, found that most had implemented management controls to reinforce the new FAR requirements and strengthen the management of interagency acquisitions.

- *New controls over the creation of new interagency contract vehicles.* In response to congressional direction and our prior recommendation, OMB established a policy framework in September 2011 to govern the creation of new interagency contract vehicles. The framework addresses concerns about potential duplication by requiring agencies to develop a thorough business case prior to establishing certain contract vehicles.

- *Improved data on interagency contracts.* OMB and the General Services Administration have taken a number of steps to address the need for better data on interagency contract vehicles. These efforts should enhance both governmentwide efforts to manage interagency contracts and agency efforts to conduct market research and negotiate better prices.

Importantly, congressional oversight sustained over several years, has been vital in addressing the issues that led this area to be designated high risk.

Removing the management of interagency contracting from the High Risk List does not mean that the federal government's use of these contracts is without challenges. But, we believe there are mechanisms in place that OMB and federal agencies can use to identify and address interagency contracting issues before they put the government at significant risk for waste, fraud, or abuse. We also will continue to monitor developments in this area.

| IRS Business Systems Modernization | The Internal Revenue Service's (IRS) Business Systems Modernization is a multi-billion dollar, highly-complex effort that involves the development and delivery of a number of modernized tax administration and internal management systems as well as core infrastructure projects that are intended to replace the agency's aging business and tax processing systems. |

In 1995, we identified serious management and technical weaknesses in IRS's modernization program that jeopardized its successful completion. We recommended many actions to fix the problems, and added IRS's modernization to our High Risk List. In 1995, we also added the agency's financial management to our High Risk List due to long-standing and pervasive problems which hampered the effective collection of revenues and precluded the preparation of auditable financial statements.[4] We combined the two issues into one high-risk area in 2005 since resolution of the most serious financial management problems depended largely on the success of the business systems modernization program.

We are removing IRS's Business Systems Modernization program from the High Risk List because of:

- *Progress in addressing weaknesses.* In our 2007, 2009, and 2011 high risk updates, we reported that IRS continued to make progress in addressing our recommendations. In January 2012, the agency delivered the initial phase of its cornerstone tax processing project and began the daily processing and posting of individual taxpayer accounts. This enhanced tax administration and improved service by enabling faster refunds for more taxpayers, allowing more timely account updates, and faster issuance of taxpayer notices. Other improvements made led us to conclude that IRS's remaining deficiencies in internal controls over information security no longer constitute a material weakness for financial reporting as of September 30, 2012.

- *Commitment to sustaining progress in the future.* In July 2011, we reported that IRS had put in place close to 80 percent of the practices needed for an effective investment management process, including all of the processes needed for effective project oversight.[5] We also reported that IRS had embarked on an effort to improve its software development practices using the Carnegie Mellon University Software Engineering Institute's Capability Maturity Model Integration (CMMI), which calls for disciplined software development and acquisition practices which are considered industry best practices. In September

---

[4]GAO, *High-Risk Series: An Overview*, HR-95-1 (Washington, D.C.: Feb. 1, 1995).

[5]GAO, *Investment Management: IRS Has a Strong Oversight Process But Needs to Improve How It Continues Funding Ongoing Investments*, GAO-11-587 (Washington, D.C.: July 20, 2011).

2012, IRS's application development organization reached CMMI maturity level 3, a high achievement by industry standards.

Throughout the years, Congress conducted oversight of the Business Systems Modernization program by, among other things, requiring that IRS submit annual expenditure plans that needed to meet certain conditions, including a review by GAO. Because of the significant progress made in addressing the high-risk area, starting in fiscal year 2012, Congress did not require the submission of an annual expenditure plan.

As with all areas removed from the High Risk List, we will continue to monitor how future events unfold.

New High-Risk Areas

To determine which federal government programs and functions should be added to the High Risk List, we consider whether the program or function is of national significance or is key to government performance and accountability. Further, we consider qualitative factors, such as whether the risk

- involves public health or safety, service delivery, national security, national defense, economic growth, or privacy or citizens' rights, or
- could result in significant impaired service, program failure, injury or loss of life, or significantly reduced economy, efficiency, or effectiveness.

In addition, we also review the exposure to loss in quantitative terms such as the value of major assets being impaired, revenue sources not being realized, or major agency assets being lost, stolen, damaged, or wasted. We also consider corrective measures planned or under way to resolve a material control weakness and the status and effectiveness of these actions.

This year, we added two new areas, delineated below, to the High Risk List based on those criteria.

Limiting the Federal Government's Fiscal Exposure by Better Managing Climate Change Risks

Climate change poses risks to many environmental and economic systems—including agriculture, infrastructure, ecosystems, and human health—and presents a significant financial risk to the federal government. The United States Global Change Research Program (USGCRP) has observed that the impacts and costliness of weather disasters will increase in significance as what are considered "rare" events become more common and intense due to climate change.[6] Among other impacts, climate change could threaten coastal areas with rising sea levels, alter agricultural productivity, and increase the intensity and frequency of severe weather events such as floods, drought, and hurricanes.

Weather-related events have cost the nation tens of billions of dollars in damages over the past decade. For example, in 2012, the administration requested $60.4 billion for Superstorm Sandy recovery efforts. These impacts pose significant financial risks for the federal government, which owns extensive infrastructure, insures property through federal flood and crop insurance programs, provides technical assistance to state and local governments, and provides emergency aid in response to natural disasters. However, the federal government is not well positioned to address this fiscal exposure, partly because of the complex, cross-cutting nature of the issue. Given these challenges and the nation's precarious fiscal condition, we have added limiting the federal government's fiscal exposure to climate change to our 2013 list of high-risk areas.[7]

Climate change adaptation—defined as adjustments to natural or human systems in response to actual or expected climate change—is a risk-management strategy to help protect vulnerable sectors and communities that might be affected by changes in the climate. For example, adaptation

---

[6]Thomas R. Karl, Jerry M. Melillo, and Thomas C. Peterson, eds. *Global Climate Change Impacts in the United States* (Cambridge University Press: 2009). USGCRP coordinates and integrates the activities of 13 federal agencies that conduct research on changes in the global environment and their implications for society. USGCRP began as a presidential initiative in 1989 and was codified in the Global Change Research Act of 1990 [Pub. L. No. 101-606, § 103 (1990)]. USGCRP-participating agencies are the Departments of Agriculture, Commerce, Defense, Energy, Interior, Health and Human Services, State, and Transportation; U.S. Agency for International Development; Environmental Protection Agency; National Aeronautics and Space Administration; the National Science Foundation; and the Smithsonian Institution.

[7]The focus of this high-risk area may evolve over time to the extent that federal climate change programs and policies change.

measures may include raising river or coastal dikes to protect infrastructure from sea level rise, building higher bridges, and increasing the capacity of storm water systems. Policymakers increasingly view climate change adaptation as a risk-management strategy to protect vulnerable sectors and communities that might be affected by changes in the climate, but, as we reported in 2009, the federal government's emerging adaptation activities were carried out in an ad hoc manner and were not well coordinated across federal agencies, let alone with state and local governments.[8]

The federal government has a number of efforts underway to decrease domestic greenhouse gas emissions, but decreasing global emissions depends in large part on cooperative international efforts. Further, according to the National Research Council and USGCRP, greenhouse gases already in the atmosphere will continue altering the climate system for many decades. As such, the impacts of climate change can be expected to increase fiscal exposure for the federal government in many areas:

- *Federal government as property owner.* The federal government owns and operates hundreds of thousands of buildings and facilities, such as defense installations, that could be affected by a changing climate. In addition, the federal government manages about 650 million acres——29 percent of the 2.27 billion acres of U.S. land—for a wide variety of purposes, such as recreation, grazing, timber, and fish and wildlife. In 2007, we recommended that that the Secretaries of Agriculture, Commerce, and the Interior develop guidance for resource managers that explains how they are expected to address the effects of climate changes, and the three departments generally agreed with the recommendation. We have ongoing work related to adapting infrastructure and the management of federal lands to a changing climate.

  Federal insurance programs. Two important federal insurance efforts—the National Flood Insurance Program (NFIP) and the Federal Crop Insurance Corporation—are based on conditions, priorities, and approaches that were established decades ago and do not account for climate change. NFIP has been on our High Risk List

---

[8]GAO, *Climate Change Adaptation: Strategic Federal Planning Could Help Government Officials Make More Informed Decisions*, GAO-10-113 (Washington, D.C.: Oct. 7, 2009).

since March 2006 because of concerns about its long-term financial solvency and related operational issues.[9] In March 2007, we reported that both of these insurance programs' exposure to weather-related losses had grown substantially, and that the agencies responsible for them had done little to develop the information necessary to understand their long-term exposure to climate change.[10] We recommended that the responsible agencies analyze the potential long-term fiscal implications of climate change and report their findings to the Congress. The agencies agreed with the recommendation and contracted with experts to study their programs' long-term exposure to climate change, but the results of the work have not yet been reported to Congress.

In addition, in June 2011, we reported that external factors continue to complicate the administration of the NFIP and affect its financial stability.[11] In particular, the Federal Emergency Management Agency (FEMA), which administers the NFIP, was not been authorized to account for long-term erosion when updating flood maps used to set premium rates for the NFIP, increasing the likelihood that premiums would not cover future losses. We suggested that Congress consider authorizing the NFIP to account for long-term flood erosion in its flood maps, and the Biggert-Waters Flood Insurance Reform Act of 2012 requires FEMA to use information on topography, coastal erosion areas, changing lake levels, future changes in sea levels, and intensity of hurricanes in updating its flood maps. While these provisions respond to our suggestion to Congress, their ultimate effectiveness will depend on their implementation by FEMA. It is too early to evaluate such efforts, but we plan to examine the NFIP in the near future.

---

[9]The potential losses generated by NFIP have created substantial financial exposure for the federal government and U.S. taxpayers. While Congress and FEMA intended that NFIP be funded with premiums collected from policyholders and not with tax dollars, the program was, by design, not actuarially sound. As of November 2012, FEMA owes the Treasury approximately $20 billion—up from $17.8 billion pre-Sandy—and had not repaid any principal on the loan since 2010.

[10]GAO, *Climate Change: Financial Risks to Federal and Private Insurers in Coming Decades Are Potentially Significant*, GAO-07-285 (Washington, D.C.: Mar. 16, 2007).

[11]GAO, *FEMA: Action Needed to Improve Administration of the National Flood Insurance Program*, GAO-11-297 (Washington, D.C.: June 9, 2011).

GAO-13-359T

- *Technical assistance to state and local governments*. The federal government invests billions of dollars annually in infrastructure projects that state and local governments prioritize and supervise. These projects have large up front capital investments and long lead times that require decisions about how to address climate change to be made well before its potential effects are discernable. We reported in October 2009 that insufficient site-specific data—such as local temperature and precipitation projections—make it hard for state and local officials to justify the current costs of adaptation efforts for potentially less certain future benefits.[12] We recommended that the appropriate entities within the Executive Office of the President develop a strategic plan for adaptation that, among other things, identifies mechanisms to increase the capacity of federal, state, and local agencies to incorporate information about current and potential climate change impacts into government decision making.

  USGCRP's 2012-2021 strategic plan for climate change science, released in April 2012, recognizes this need by identifying enhanced information management and sharing as a key objective, and USGCRP is undertaking several actions designed to better coordinate use and application of federal climate science. We have ongoing work related to these issues. In addition, gaps in satellite coverage, which could occur as soon as 2014, are expected to affect the continuity of climate and space weather measurements important to developing the information needed by state and local officials.[13] According to National Oceanic and Atmospheric Administration program officials, a satellite data gap would result in less accurate and timely weather forecasts and warnings of extreme events—such as hurricanes, storm surges and floods. We have concluded that the potential gap in weather satellite data is a high-risk area and added it to the High Risk List this year as well.

- *Disaster aid*. In the event of a major disaster, federal funding for response and recovery comes from the Disaster Relief Fund managed by FEMA and disaster aid programs of other participating

---

[12]GAO-10-113.

[13]See, for example, GAO, *Environmental Satellites: Focused Attention Needed to Mitigate Program Risks*, GAO-12-841T (Washington, D.C.: June 27, 2012), and *Environmental Satellites: Strategy Needed to Sustain Critical Climate and Space Weather Measurements*, GAO-10-456 (Washington, D.C.: Apr. 27, 2010).

federal agencies. The federal government does not budget for these costs and runs the risk of facing a large fiscal exposure at any time. We reported in September 2012 that disaster declarations have increased over recent decades to a record of 98 in fiscal year 2011 compared with 65 in 2004. Over that period, FEMA obligated more than $80 billion in federal assistance for disasters.[14] We found that FEMA has had difficulty implementing longstanding plans to assess national preparedness capabilities and that FEMA's indicator for determining whether to recommend that a jurisdiction receive disaster assistance does not accurately reflect the ability of state and local governments to respond to disasters.[15] In September 2012, we recommended, among other things, that FEMA develop a methodology to more accurately assess a jurisdiction's capability to respond to and recover from a disaster without federal assistance. FEMA concurred with this recommendation.

The federal government would be better positioned to respond to the risks posed by climate change if federal efforts were more coordinated and directed toward common goals. In 2009, we recommended that the appropriate entities within the Executive Office of the President develop a strategic plan to guide the nation's efforts to adapt to climate change, including the establishment of clear roles, responsibilities, and working relationships among federal, state, and local governments.[16],[17] Some actions have subsequently been taken, including the development of an

---

[14]GAO, *Federal Disaster Assistance: Improved Criteria Needed to Assess a Jurisdiction's Capability to Respond and Recover on Its Own*, GAO-12-838 (Washington, D.C.: Sept. 12, 2012).

[15]GAO, *Managing Preparedness Grants and Assessing National Capabilities*, GAO-12-526T (Washington, D.C.: Mar. 20, 2012). See also GAO, *Disaster Response: Criteria for Developing and Validating Effective Response Plans*, GAO-10-969T (Washington, D.C.: Sept. 22, 2010).

[16]The Council on Environmental Quality coordinates federal environmental efforts and the development of environmental policies and initiatives. The Office of Science and Technology Policy was established by statute in 1976 to serve as a source of scientific and technological analysis and judgment for the President with respect to major policies, plans, and programs of the federal government, among other things.

[17]GAO-10-113.

interagency climate change adaptation task force.[18] However, a 2012 National Research Council report states that while the task force has convened representatives of relevant agencies and programs, it has no mechanisms for making or enforcing important decisions and priorities.[19]

In May 2011, we found no coherent strategic government-wide approach to climate change funding and that federal officials do not have a shared understanding of strategic government-wide priorities.[20] At that time, we recommended that the appropriate entities within the Executive Office of the President clearly establish federal strategic climate change priorities, including the roles and responsibilities of the key federal entities, taking into consideration the full range of climate-related activities within the federal government. The relevant federal entities have not directly addressed this recommendation.

Federal agencies have made some progress toward better organizing across agencies, within agencies, and among different levels of government; however, the increasing fiscal exposure for the federal government calls for more comprehensive and systematic strategic planning including, but not limited to, the following:

- A government-wide strategic approach with strong leadership and the authority to manage climate change risks that encompasses the entire range of related federal activities and addresses all key elements of strategic planning.

---

[18]Executive Order 13514 on Federal Leadership in Environmental, Energy, and Economic Performance calls for federal agencies to participate actively in the already existing Interagency Climate Change Adaptation Task Force. The task force, which began meeting in Spring 2009, is co-chaired by the Council on Environmental Quality, the National Oceanic and Atmospheric Administration, and the Office of Science and Technology Policy, and includes representatives from more than 20 federal agencies and executive branch offices. The task force was formed to assess key steps needed to help the federal government understand and adapt to climate change.

[19]National Research Council, Committee on a National Strategy for Advancing Climate Modeling, Board on Atmospheric Studies and Climate, Division on Earth and Life Sciences, *A National Strategy for Advancing Climate Modeling* (Washington, D.C.: 2012).

[20]GAO, *Climate Change: Improvements Needed to Clarify National Priorities and Better Align Them with Federal Funding Decisions*, GAO-11-317 (Washington, D.C.: May 20, 2011).

- More information to understand and manage federal insurance programs' long-term exposure to climate change and analyze the potential impacts of an increase in the frequency or severity of weather-related events on their operations.

- A government-wide approach for providing (1) the best available climate-related data for making decisions at the state and local level and (2) assistance for translating available climate-related data into information that officials need to make decisions.

- Potential gaps in satellite data need to be effectively addressed.

- Improved criteria for assessing a jurisdiction's capability to respond and recover from a disaster without federal assistance, and to better apply lessons from past experience when developing disaster cost estimates.

Additional information on *Limiting the Federal Government's Fiscal Exposure by Better Managing Climate Change Risks* is provided in the 2013 high risk update report.

Mitigating Gaps in Weather Satellite Data

For 2013, we are designating a new high-risk area—Mitigating Gaps in Weather Satellite Data. We and others—including an independent review team reporting to the Department of Commerce and the department's Inspector General—have raised concerns that problems and delays on environmental satellite acquisition programs will result in gaps in the continuity of critical satellite data used in weather forecasts and warnings. The importance of such data was recently highlighted by the advance warnings of the path, timing, and intensity of Superstorm Sandy.

Since the 1960s, the United States has used both polar-orbiting and geostationary satellites to observe the earth and its land, oceans, atmosphere, and space environments. Polar-orbiting satellites constantly circle the earth in an almost north-south orbit providing global coverage of environmental conditions that affect the weather and climate. As the earth rotates beneath it, each polar-orbiting satellite views the entire earth's surface twice a day. In contrast, geostationary satellites maintain a fixed position relative to the earth from a high-level orbit of about 22,300 miles in space. Used in combination with ground, sea, and airborne observing systems, both types of satellites have become an indispensable part of monitoring and forecasting weather and climate. For example, polar-orbiting satellites provide the data that go into numerical weather prediction models, which are a primary tool for forecasting weather days in advance—including forecasting the path and intensity of hurricanes and tropical storms. Geostationary satellites provide frequently-updated graphical images that are used to identify current weather patterns and provide short-term warnings.

Polar-orbiting Satellites

For more than 40 years, the United States has operated two separate operational polar-orbiting meteorological satellites systems: the Polar-orbiting Operational Environmental Satellite series, which is managed by National Oceanic and Atmospheric Administration (NOAA)—a component of the Department of Commerce; and the Defense Meteorological Satellite Program (DMSP), which is managed by the Air Force. The government also relies on data from a European satellite program, called the Meteorological Operational (MetOp) satellite series. These satellites are positioned so that they cross the equator in the early morning, midmorning, and early afternoon in order to obtain regular updates throughout the day.

With the expectation that combining the two separate U.S. polar satellite programs would result in sizable cost savings, a May 1994 Presidential Decision Directive required NOAA and DOD to converge the two programs into a single new satellite acquisition, which became the National Polar-orbiting Operational Environmental Satellite System (NPOESS). However, in the years that followed, NPOESS encountered significant technical challenges in sensor development and experienced program cost growth and schedule delays, in part due to problems in the program's management structure. After several restructurings and recurring challenges, in February 2010, the Executive Office of the President's Office of Science and Technology Policy announced that NOAA and DOD would no longer jointly procure NPOESS; instead, each agency would plan and acquire its own satellite system. Specifically, NOAA, with support from the National Aeronautics and Space Administration (NASA), would be responsible for the afternoon orbit, and DOD would be responsible for the early morning orbit. The U.S. partnership with the European satellite agency for data from the midmorning orbit would continue as planned.

Subsequently, NOAA initiated its replacement program, the Joint Polar Satellite System (JPSS). JPSS consists of a demonstration satellite—called the Suomi National Polar-orbiting Partnership (NPP)—launched in October 2011; two satellites, with at least five instruments planned for each, to be launched by March 2017 and December 2022, respectively; two stand-alone satellites to accommodate three additional instruments; and ground systems for the entire program. The program is currently estimated to cost $12.9 billion. In June 2012, we reported that NOAA and NASA made progress in establishing the JPSS program and in launching and operating the demonstration satellite, but noted that program officials expect there to be a gap in satellite observations before the first JPSS satellite is launched.

Specifically, NOAA officials anticipate a gap in the afternoon orbit from 18 to 24 months between the time that NPP reaches the end of its lifespan and when the first JPSS satellite is fully ready for operational use. We identified other scenarios where the gap could last from 17 to 53 months. For example, the gap would be 17 months if NPP lasts 5 years until October 2016 and JPSS is launched as planned in March 2017 and undergoes a 12-month on-orbit checkout before it is fully operational. Alternatively, if NPP lasts only 3 years—which NASA engineers consider possible due to poor workmanship in the fabrication of the instruments— and JPSS launches 1 year later than currently planned, the gap in satellite observations could reach 53 months.

After NPOESS was disbanded, DOD also began planning its own follow-on polar satellite program. However, it halted work in early 2012, since it still has two legacy DMSP satellites in storage that will be launched as needed to maintain observations in the early morning orbit. The agency currently plans to launch its two remaining satellites in 2014 and 2020. Moreover, DOD is working to identify alternatives to meet its future environmental satellite requirements. However, in June 2012, we reported that there is a possibility of satellite data gaps in DOD's early morning orbit. The two remaining DMSP satellites may not work as intended because they were built in the late 1990s and will be quite old by the time they are launched. If the satellites do not perform as expected, a data gap in the early morning orbit could occur as early as 2014.

Satellite data gaps in the morning or afternoon polar orbits would lead to less accurate and timely weather forecasting; as a result, advanced warning of extreme events would be affected. Such extreme events could include hurricanes, storm surges, and floods. For example, the National Weather Service performed case studies to demonstrate how its forecasts would have been affected if there were no polar satellite data in the afternoon orbit, and noted that its forecasts for the "Snowmaggedon" winter storm that hit the Mid-Atlantic coast in February 2010 would have predicted a less intense storm further east, with about half of the precipitation at 3, 4, and 5 days before the event. Specifically, the models would have under-forecasted the amount of snow by at least 10 inches. Similarly, a European weather organization[21] recently reported that NOAA's forecasts of Superstorm Sandy's track could have been hundreds of miles off without polar-orbiting satellites: rather than identifying the New Jersey landfall within 30 miles 4 days before landfall, the models would have shown the storm remaining at sea.

In June 2012, we reported that while NOAA officials communicated publicly and often about the risk of a polar satellite data gap, the agency had not established plans to mitigate the gap. At the time, NOAA officials stated that the agency would continue to use existing satellites as long as they provide data and that there were no viable alternatives to the JPSS program. However, our report noted that a more comprehensive mitigation plan was essential since it is possible that other governmental, commercial, or foreign satellites could supplement the polar satellite data. For example, other nations continue to launch polar-orbiting weather satellites to acquire data such as sea surface temperatures, sea surface winds, and water vapor. Also, over the next few years, NASA plans to launch satellites that will collect information on precipitation and soil moisture. Because it could take time to adapt ground systems to receive, process, and disseminate an alternative satellite's data, we noted that any delays in establishing mitigation plans could leave the agency little time to leverage its alternatives. We recommended that NOAA establish mitigation plans for pending satellite gaps in the afternoon orbit as well as potential gaps in the early morning orbit.

In September 2012, the Under Secretary of Commerce for Oceans and Atmosphere (who is also the NOAA Administrator) reported that NOAA had several actions under way to address polar satellite data gaps, including (1) an investigation on how to maximize the life of the demonstration satellite, (2) an investigation on how to accelerate the development of the second JPSS satellite, and (3) the development of a mitigation plan to address potential data gaps until the first JPSS satellite becomes operational. The Under Secretary also directed NOAA's Assistant Secretary to, by mid-October 2012, establish a contract to conduct an enterprise-wide examination of contingency options and to

---

[21]The European Centre for Medium Range Weather Forecasts is an independent, intergovernmental organization supported by 34 European nations, providing global medium-to-extended range forecasts.

develop a written, descriptive, end-to-end plan that considers the entire flow of data from possible alternative sensors through data assimilation and on to forecast model performance. In October 2012, NOAA issued a mitigation plan for a potential gap in the afternoon orbit, between the current polar satellite and the first JPSS satellite. The plan identifies and prioritizes options for obtaining critical observations, including alternative satellite data sources and improvements to data assimilation in models. It also lists technical, programmatic, and management steps needed to implement these options.

However, these plans are only the beginning. The agency must make difficult decisions on which steps it will implement to ensure that its mitigation plans are viable when needed. For example, NOAA must make decisions about (1) whether and how to extend support for legacy satellite systems so that their data might be available if needed, (2) how much time and resources to invest in improving satellite models so that they assimilate data from alternative sources, (3) whether to pursue international agreements for access to additional satellite systems and how best to resolve any security issues with the foreign data, (4) when and how to test the value and integration of alternative data sources, and (5) how these preliminary mitigation plans will be integrated with the agency's broader end-to-end plans for sustaining weather forecasting capabilities. NOAA must also identify time frames for when these decisions will be made. We have ongoing work assessing NOAA's efforts to limit and mitigate potential polar satellite data gaps.

Geostationary Satellites

Geostationary environmental satellites transmit frequently updated images of the weather currently affecting the United States to every national weather forecast office in the country. These are the satellite images that the public often sees on television news programs. NOAA plans to have its $10.9 billion Geostationary Operational Environmental Satellite-R (GOES-R) series replace the current fleet of geostationary satellites, which will begin to reach the end of their useful lives in 2015. The GOES-R program has undergone a series of changes since 2006 and now consists of four geostationary satellites and a ground system. However, problems with instrument and ground system development caused a 19-month delay in completing the program's preliminary design review, which occurred in February 2012. In June 2012, we reported that GOES-R schedules were not fully reliable and that they could contribute to delays in satellite launch dates. Program officials acknowledged that the likelihood of meeting the October 2015 launch date was 48 percent.

While NOAA's policy is to have two operational satellites and one backup satellite in orbit at all times, continued delays in the launch of the first GOES-R satellite could lead to a gap in satellite coverage. This policy proved useful in December 2008 and again in September 2012 when the agency experienced problems with one of its operational satellites, but was able to move its backup satellite into place until the problems were resolved. However, beginning in April 2015, NOAA expects to have only two operational satellites and no backup satellite in orbit until GOES-R is launched and completes an estimated 6-month post-launch test period. As a result, there could be a year or more gap during which time a backup satellite would not be available. If NOAA were to experience a problem with either of its operational satellites before GOES-R is in orbit and operational, it would need to rely on older satellites that are beyond their expected operational lives and may not be fully functional. Any further delays in the launch of the first satellite in the GOES-R program would likely increase the risk of a gap in satellite coverage.

In September 2010, we reported that NOAA had not established adequate continuity plans for its geostationary satellites. Specifically, in the event of a satellite failure, with no backup available, NOAA planned to reduce its operations to a single satellite and if available, rely on a satellite from a foreign nation. However, the agency did not have plans that included processes, procedures, and resources needed to transition to a single or a foreign satellite. Without such plans, there would be an increased risk that users would lose access to critical data. We recommended that NOAA develop and document continuity plans for the operation of geostationary satellites that included implementation procedures, resources, staff roles, and timetables needed to transition to a single satellite, a foreign satellite, or other solution. In September 2011, NOAA developed an initial continuity plan that generally includes these elements. Specifically, NOAA's plan identified steps it would take in transitioning to a single or foreign satellite; the amount of time this transition would take; roles of product area leads; and resources such as imaging product schedules, disk imagery frequency, and staff to execute the changes. In December 2012, NOAA issued an updated plan that provides additional contingency scenarios.

- However, it is not evident that critical steps have been implemented, including simulating continuity situations and working with the user community to account for differences in products under different continuity scenarios. These steps are critical for NOAA to move forward in documenting the processes it will take to implement its contingency plans. Once these activities are completed, NOAA should update its contingency plan to provide more details on its contingency scenarios, associated time frames, and any preventative actions it is taking to minimize the possibility of a gap. We have ongoing work assessing NOAA's actions to ensure that its plans are viable and that continuity procedures are in place and have been tested. Additional information on Mitigating Gaps in Weather Satellite Data is provided in our high-risk update report.

High Risk Areas Narrowing Due to Progress

Since our 2011 update, sufficient progress has been made to narrow the scope of the following three areas.

Management of Federal Oil and Gas Resources

In 2011, we added the Department of the Interior's (Interior) management of oil and gas on leased federal lands and waters to GAO's High Risk List for three reasons; (1) Interior did not have reasonable assurance that it was collecting its share of revenue from oil and gas produced on federal lands; (2) Interior was unable to hire, train, and retain sufficient staff to provide oversight and management of oil and gas operations on federal lands and waters; and (3) Interior was reorganizing its oversight of offshore oil and gas activities in the immediate aftermath of the Deepwater Horizon incident. Since 2011, sufficient progress has been made in one of these three areas—Interior's reorganization of its oversight of offshore oil and gas activities—but Interior's revenue collection and human capital challenges remain a concern.

The explosion onboard the Deepwater Horizon and oil spill in the Gulf of Mexico in April 2010 emphasized the importance of Interior's management of permitting and inspections to ensure operational and environmental safety. In 2011, Interior undertook a substantial reorganization of its oversight of offshore oil and gas activities that included establishing three new bureaus and separating revenue collection and oversight functions. At that time, we raised concerns about Interior's ability to continue to perform these functions while undertaking this reorganization. In July 2012, we concluded that Interior had fundamentally completed its reorganization. However, Interior continues to face challenges in collecting the appropriate amount of royalties from oil and gas produced on federal lands and waters. We have recommended that Interior reassess its revenue collection policies and processes and correct problems with its data on oil and gas production, and Interior is working to implement a number of these recommendations.

We are reviewing Interior's revenue collection practices and will evaluate, among other things, Interior's progress in implementing these recommendations. Interior also continues to face problems in hiring, training, and retaining staff at the bureaus responsible for managing federal oil and gas resources, potentially placing both the environment and royalties at risk. We are reviewing Interior's human capital challenges, focusing on the causes of these challenges and the actions Interior is taking to address them.

Department of Energy's Contract Management for the National Nuclear Security Administration and Office of Environmental Management

To recognize progress at the Department of Energy (DOE) on the National Nuclear Security Administration's (NNSA) and Office of Environmental Management's (EM) execution of nonmajor projects—projects with values of less than $750 million—we are shifting the focus of its high-risk designation more to major contracts and projects executed by NNSA and EM, those contracts and projects with values of $750 million or greater. These contracts include those for management and operating contracts for national laboratories and nuclear production plants—such as Los Alamos National Laboratory—that are government owned and contractor operated, as well as for capital asset projects—such as the Hanford Tank Waste Treatment and Immobilization Plant under construction in Hanford, Washington, and the Mixed Oxide Fuel Fabrication Facility under construction near Aiken, South Carolina—projects that are currently estimated to cost $13.4 billion and $4.9 billion respectively with cost increases anticipated.

Two of our reviews completed in 2012 focused on nonmajor projects found that these projects were being completed in large part, although additional and sustained attention by DOE is needed to adequately set and document performance baselines and further demonstrate that these actions result in improved performance. These reports included recommendations to DOE to clearly define, document, and track the scope, cost, and completion date targets for each of its projects, as required by DOE's project management order. DOE agreed with these recommendations. With further monitoring of this area to ensure that progress is sustained, coupled with continued efforts and commitment by top leadership to address contract and project management weaknesses, nonmajor project performance issues will have been sufficiently addressed.

Significant challenges remain for the successful execution of major projects. NNSA is tasked with modernizing the nation's aging nuclear weapons production facilities, a difficult effort that will take years and cost billions of dollars. EM faces ongoing complex and long-term challenges in removing radioactive and hazardous chemical contaminants—left over from decades of weapons production—from soil, groundwater, and facilities. Billions of dollars have already been spent, and will continue to be spent over the coming decades to treat and dispose of this waste. NNSA and EM are currently managing 10 major projects with combined estimated costs totaling as much as $65.7 billion.

As part of this high-risk update, we examined these 10 projects but were only able to analyze changes in schedule estimates for 5 projects and cost estimates for 7 projects because of limitations in the data. For these projects, we determined that DOE has added as much as 38.5 years to their initial schedules and $16.5 billion to original cost estimates with further delays and cost increases anticipated. For example, since we reported in February 2011 that NNSA's project to design and construct a new Uranium Processing Facility at the Y-12 National Security Complex had experienced nearly seven-fold cost growth from its 2004 estimate to the current estimate of between $4.2 billion and $6.5 billion, the facility will be redesigned to correct issues concerning processing equipment with the potential for significant additional cost and schedule delay. NNSA and EM will remain on the High Risk List until DOE can consistently demonstrate that recent changes to policies and processes are resulting in improved performance on major projects.

Strengthening Department of Homeland Security Management Functions

In 2003, we designated implementing and transforming the Department of Homeland Security (DHS) as high risk because DHS had to transform 22 agencies—several with major management challenges—into one department. Further, failure to effectively address DHS's management and mission risks could have serious consequences for U.S. national and economic security. Given the significant effort required to build and integrate a new department as large and complex as DHS, our initial high risk designation focused on the department's initial transformation and subsequent implementation efforts, to include associated management and programmatic challenges.

Over the past 10 years, the focus of this high-risk area has evolved in tandem with DHS's maturation and evolution. The overriding tenet has consistently remained the department's ability to build a single, cohesive and effective department that is greater than the sum of its parts—a goal that requires effective collaboration and integration of its various components and management functions. In 2007, in reporting on DHS's progress since its creation, as well as in our 2009 high risk update, we noted that DHS had made more progress in implementing its range of missions than in its management functions, and that continued work was needed to address an array of programmatic and management challenges.

DHS's initial focus on mission implementation was understandable given the critical homeland security needs facing the nation after the department's establishment, and the challenges posed by its creation, integration and transformation. As DHS continued to mature, and as we reported in our assessment of DHS's progress and challenges 10 years after 9/11, we found that the department implemented key homeland security operations and achieved important goals in many areas to create and strengthen a foundation to reach its potential.[22] However, we also identified that more work remained for DHS to address weaknesses in its operational and implementation efforts, and to strengthen the efficiency and effectiveness of those efforts. We further reported that continuing weaknesses in DHS's management functions had been a key theme impacting the department's implementation efforts. Recognizing DHS's progress in transformation and mission implementation, our 2011 high risk update focused on the continued need to strengthen DHS's management functions (acquisition, information technology, financial management, and human capital) and integrate those functions within and across the department, as well as the impact of these challenges on the department's ability to effectively and efficiently carry out its missions.

While challenges remain for DHS to address across its range of missions, the department has made considerable progress in transforming its original component agencies into a single cabinet-level department and positioning itself to achieve its full potential. Important strides have also been made in strengthening the department's management functions and in integrating those functions across the department, particularly in recent years. For example, DHS has chartered eight Centers of Excellence to

---

[22]GAO, *Department of Homeland Security: Progress Made and Work Remaining in Implementing Homeland Security Missions 10 Years after 9/11*, GAO-11-881 (Washington, D.C.: Sept. 7, 2011). This report addressed DHS's progress in implementing its homeland security missions since it began operations, work remaining, and issues affecting implementation efforts. Drawing from over 1,000 GAO reports and congressional testimony issued related to DHS programs and operations, and approximately 1,500 recommendations made to strengthen mission and management implementation, this report addressed progress and remaining challenges in such areas as border security and immigration, transportation security, and emergency management, among others.

enhance component acquisition capabilities, defined and begun to implement a vision for a tiered governance structure intended to improve its information technology program and portfolio management, obtained a qualified audit opinion on its fiscal year 2012 financial statements, and issued a workforce strategy and a revised Workforce Planning Guide to help the department address its human capital challenges and plan for its workforce needs.

However, DHS still has considerable work ahead in many areas. For example, in September 2012, we reported that most of DHS's major acquisition programs continue to cost more than expected, take longer to deploy than planned, or deliver less capability than promised. We identified 42 programs that experienced cost growth or schedule slips, or both, with 16 of the programs' costs increasing from a total of $19.7 billion in 2008 to $52.2 billion in 2011—an aggregate increase of 166 percent. Further, while DHS has defined and begun to implement a vision for a tiered governance structure to improve information technology (IT) management, we reported in July 2012 that the governance structure covers less than 20 percent (about 16 of 80) of DHS's major IT investments and 3 of its 13 portfolios. DHS has also been unable to obtain an audit opinion on its internal controls over financial reporting, and needs to obtain and sustain unqualified audit opinions for at least two consecutive years on the department-wide financial statements. Finally, federal surveys have consistently found that DHS employees are less satisfied with their jobs than the government-wide average. Key to addressing the department's management challenges is DHS demonstrating the ability to achieve sustained progress across the 31 actions and outcomes we identified as needed to address the high-risk designation, to which DHS agreed. As shown in table 1, we believe DHS has fully addressed 6, mostly addressed 2, partially addressed 16, and initiated 7 of the 31 key actions and outcomes.

Table 1: Assessment of DHS's Progress in Addressing Key Actions and Outcomes

Key outcomes	Fully addressed[a]	Mostly addressed[b]	Partially addressed[c]	Initiated[d]	Total
Acquisition management			2	3	5
IT management	1	1	4		6
Financial management	2		3	4	9
Human capital management		1	6		7
Management integration	3		1		4
Total	6	2	16	7	31

Source: GAO analysis of DHS documents, interviews, and prior GAO reports.

[a]"Fully addressed": outcome is fully addressed.

[b]"Mostly addressed": progress is significant and a small amount of work remains.

[c]"Partially addressed": progress is measurable, but significant work remains.

[d]"Initiated": activities have been initiated to address outcome, but it is too early to report progress.

To more fully address GAO's high-risk designation, continued progress is needed in order to mitigate the risks that management weaknesses pose to mission accomplishment and the efficient and effective use of the department's resources. In particular, the department needs to demonstrate continued progress in implementing and strengthening key management initiatives and addressing corrective actions and outcomes. Therefore, we are narrowing the scope of the high-risk area and changing the name from *Implementing and Transforming the Department of Homeland Security* to *Strengthening the Department of Homeland Security Management Functions* to reflect this focus.

Modified High-Risk Area

One area—Modernizing the Outdated U.S. Financial Regulatory System—has been modified due to changing circumstances to include the Federal Housing Administration (FHA). To reflect these changing circumstances, the name of the area has been changed as well.

Modernizing the U.S. Financial Regulatory System and Federal Role in Housing Finance

We first designated this area as high risk in 2009 due to the urgent need to reform the fragmented and outdated U.S. financial regulatory system. As detailed in our 2013 high risk update report, many actions are underway to implement oversight by new regulatory bodies and new requirements for market participants, although many rulemakings remain unfinished. Among the additional actions needed are resolving the role of the two housing-related government-sponsored enterprises (GSE)—Fannie Mae and Freddie Mac—that continue operating under government conservatorships. However, a new challenge for the markets has also evolved as the decline in private sector participation in housing finance that began with the 2007-2009 financial crisis has resulted in much greater activity by FHA, whose single-family loan insurance portfolio has grown from about $300 billion in 2007 to more than $1.1 trillion in 2012. Although required to maintain capital reserves equal to at least 2 percent of its portfolio, FHA's capital reserves have fallen below this level, due partly to increases in projected defaults on the loans it has insured. As a result, we are modifying this high-risk area to include FHA and acknowledge the need for actions beyond those already taken to help restore FHA's financial soundness and define its future role. One such action would be to determine the economic conditions that FHA's primary insurance fund would be expected to withstand without drawing on the Treasury. Recent events suggest that the 2-percent capital requirement may not be adequate to avoid the need for Treasury support under severe stress scenarios. Additionally, actions to reform GSEs and to implement mortgage market reforms in the Dodd-Frank Act will need to consider the potential impacts on FHA's risk exposure.

Progress on Remaining High-Risk Areas

There has been notable progress on the vast majority of the issues that remain on the High Risk List. The nation cannot afford to allow problems to persist. Addressing high-risk problems can save billions of dollars each year. Several areas on the High Risk List illustrate both the challenges of addressing difficult and tenacious high-risk problems and the opportunities for savings that can accrue if progress is made to address high-risk problems.

Protecting Public Health through Enhanced Oversight of Medical Products

Congress, the administration, and the Food and Drug Administration (FDA) have all taken actions to improve the agency's oversight of medical products—drugs, biologics, and medical devices—marketed in the United States. The recently enacted Food and Drug Administration Safety and Innovation Act of 2012 (Public Law 112-144) included several provisions to enhance FDA's oversight that reflects recommendations we have made. For example, the law directed FDA to take a risk-based approach in selecting foreign drug establishments for inspections, as we recommended in September 2008. It also required FDA to improve oversight of medical device recalls by directing FDA to take actions consistent with the recommendations in our June 2011 report. In addition, the law addressed the problem of drug shortages by requiring manufacturers to advise FDA of any changes that could affect the supply of their drugs, as we suggested in November 2011. Further, the President issued an Executive Order in October 2011 that instructs FDA to expedite review of applications to market drugs that would help to prevent or resolve shortages.

FDA has also taken important steps. For example, as we recommended, FDA developed an evidence-based estimate of its resource needs and improved the quality of some of the data it uses to manage its foreign drug inspection program. This is important progress. Nevertheless, we believe that FDA must do more to bolster its oversight of medical products. FDA needs to fully implement the provisions in the Food and Drug Administration Safety and Innovation Act cited above and address other outstanding concerns. Specifically, FDA needs to:

- strengthen its Drug Shortage Program by assessing program resources, systematically tracking data on shortages, considering the availability of medically necessary drugs as a strategic priority, and developing relevant results-oriented performance metrics to gauge the agency's response to shortages;
- improve oversight of medical device recalls by routinely assessing information on device recalls, clarifying procedures for conducting recalls, developing criteria for evaluating the effectiveness of recalls, and documenting the agency's basis for terminating individual recalls;
- implement the Safe Medical Devices Act of 1990;
- conduct more inspections of foreign establishments manufacturing medical products for the U.S. market and utilize new authority to take a risk-based approach in selecting foreign drug establishments to ensure that they are inspected at a frequency comparable to domestic establishments with similar characteristics;
- emphasize the importance of timely medical product reviews, particularly for medical devices; and
- track applications to market medical products for children.

Pension Benefit Guaranty Corporation Insurance Programs

The Pension Benefit Guaranty Corporation (PBGC) insures the pension benefits of 43 million American workers and retirees participating in nearly 26,000 private sector defined benefit plans through its single-employer and multiemployer insurance programs. Because of long-term challenges related to PBGC's governance and funding structure, PBGC's financial future is uncertain. At the end of fiscal year 2012, PBGC's net accumulated financial deficit was $34 billion—an increase of more than $23 billion from the end of fiscal year 2008.

Both Congress and PBGC have taken significant steps to address many of our concerns with the agency's overall management and governance structure, reflecting increased top-level attention to the challenges facing this agency. In July 2012, the Moving Ahead for Progress in the 21st Century Act (MAP-21) became law, with several provisions pertaining to PBGC.[23] These measures called for stabilizing sponsors' pension contribution requirements, adjusting premium rates, as well as strengthening PBGC's governance in various ways. For example, the law calls for PBGC's Board of Directors to meet more regularly, four times a year; PBGC's Inspector General to report to the Board; creation of new positions for a risk management officer and a participant and plan sponsor advocate; an independent peer review of PBGC's insurance modeling system, to be conducted annually; and a study to be conducted by the National Academy of Public Administration Association on possible changes to PBGC's governance structure. We have long recommended that the composition of PBGC's board—currently made up of the Secretaries of the Treasury, Commerce, and Labor—be expanded to include additional members with diverse knowledge and expertise useful to PBGC's mission.

PBGC also has taken steps to address several areas of weakness noted in our previous reports. For example, to improve its asset management, PBGC issued a new investment policy statement in May 2011 and has subsequently aligned its portfolio with these new objectives. To enhance understanding of potential reforms to its premium structure, PBGC modeled various options for adjusting premiums to better reflect the risk of future claims. To strengthen the accountability of its contract management, PBGC implemented new practices requiring documentation of the decision to use contractors instead of federal employees, annual reviews of contract files, and evaluation of staff's performance of contract monitoring duties. However, despite these efforts, certain challenges related to PBGC's governance and funding structure remain. To improve the stability of PBGC's insurance programs, we believe further congressional action should be considered with respect to: expanding and diversifying PBGC's board, redesigning PBGC's premium structure, strengthening pension plan funding requirements, and developing a strategy for PBGC's long-term financial solvency as the defined benefit sector continues to decline.

---

[23]Pub. L. No.112-141, 126 Stat. 405, 846-864.

DOD Supply Chain Management

DOD has taken positive steps to address weaknesses in its supply chain, particularly in the management of spare parts inventories. Our prior work reviewing spare parts management at the military services and the Defense Logistics Agency (DLA) identified ineffective and inefficient inventory management practices. Problems with accurately forecasting demand for spare parts have resulted in DOD purchasing and storing billions of dollars worth of excess inventory. For example, DOD's most recent available data shows that in September 2011 it had $9.2 billion worth of on-hand excess inventory, categorized for potential reuse or disposal, and $523 million worth of on-order excess inventory, already purchased but likely to be excess due to changes in requirements. In response to a provision of the National Defense Authorization Act for fiscal year 2010, DOD submitted a corrective action plan to Congress in November 2010 aimed at reducing excess inventory by improving inventory management practices. DOD established overarching goals in the plan to reduce on-hand excess inventory and on-order excess inventory. Additionally, DOD developed actions to improve inventory management in nine key areas, including improving demand forecasting for spare parts.

We reported in 2012 that DOD had made progress in implementing its inventory improvement plan and was tracking reductions to its excess inventory. With respect to on-hand excess inventory, DOD has met its fiscal year 2012 target of having no more than 10 percent of its inventory categorized as on-hand excess. Also, DOD reported that from fiscal years 2009 to 2011 it had reduced on-order excess inventory by approximately $632 million—a reduction that achieved its initial target 4 years early. However, DOD continues to maintain significant quantities of excess inventory and its plan to improve inventory management practices runs through 2015. As implementation continues, DOD needs to monitor its progress in achieving the targets for on-order and on-hand excess inventory and update the targets, as necessary, to ensure the department has challenging, yet achievable targets to guide continued improvement. Moreover, challenges remain in improving demand forecasting; accelerating the use of modeling to determine the optimal number and types of parts needed at the wholesale and retail levels to achieve readiness and cost goals; and implementing revised DOD guidance outlining the processes and procedures for retaining inventory. As it implements the remainder of its plan, DOD will need to address these areas and demonstrate sustained progress in implementing corrective measures and achieving results.

Sustaining Attention on High-Risk Programs

Overall, the government continues to take high-risk problems seriously and is making long-needed progress toward correcting them. Congress has acted to address several individual high-risk areas through hearings and legislation. GAO's high-risk update and high risk website, http://www.gao.gov/highrisk/, can help inform the oversight agenda for the 113th Congress and guide efforts of the administration and agencies to improve government performance and reduce waste and risks. In support of Congress and to further progress to address high risk issues, GAO continues to review efforts and make recommendations to address high risk areas problems. As an example, today we are issuing our review of the nation's overall cybersecurity strategy.[24] Continued perseverance in addressing high-risk areas will ultimately yield significant benefits.

Thank you, Mr. Chairman, Ranking Member Cummings, and Members of the Committee. This concludes my testimony. I would be pleased to answer any questions.

For further information on this testimony, please contact J. Christopher Mihm at (202) 512-6806 or mihmj@gao.gov. Contact points for the individual high-risk areas are listed in the report and on our high-risk web site. Contact points for our Congressional Relations and Public Affairs offices may be found on the last page of this statement.

---

[24]GAO, *Cybersecurity: National Strategy, Roles, and Responsibilities Need to Be Better Defined and More Effectively Implemented*, GAO-13-187, (Washington, D.C.: Feb. 14, 2013).

GAO's Mission	The Government Accountability Office, the audit, evaluation, and investigative arm of Congress, exists to support Congress in meeting its constitutional responsibilities and to help improve the performance and accountability of the federal government for the American people. GAO examines the use of public funds; evaluates federal programs and policies; and provides analyses, recommendations, and other assistance to help Congress make informed oversight, policy, and funding decisions. GAO's commitment to good government is reflected in its core values of accountability, integrity, and reliability.
Obtaining Copies of GAO Reports and Testimony	The fastest and easiest way to obtain copies of GAO documents at no cost is through GAO's website (http://www.gao.gov). Each weekday afternoon, GAO posts on its website newly released reports, testimony, and correspondence. To have GAO e-mail you a list of newly posted products, go to http://www.gao.gov and select "E-mail Updates."
Order by Phone	The price of each GAO publication reflects GAO's actual cost of production and distribution and depends on the number of pages in the publication and whether the publication is printed in color or black and white. Pricing and ordering information is posted on GAO's website, http://www.gao.gov/ordering.htm. Place orders by calling (202) 512-6000, toll free (866) 801-7077, or TDD (202) 512-2537. Orders may be paid for using American Express, Discover Card, MasterCard, Visa, check, or money order. Call for additional information.
Connect with GAO	Connect with GAO on Facebook, Flickr, Twitter, and YouTube. Subscribe to our RSS Feeds or E-mail Updates. Listen to our Podcasts. Visit GAO on the web at www.gao.gov.
To Report Fraud, Waste, and Abuse in Federal Programs	Contact: Website: http://www.gao.gov/fraudnet/fraudnet.htm E-mail: fraudnet@gao.gov Automated answering system: (800) 424-5454 or (202) 512-7470
Congressional Relations	Katherine Siggerud, Managing Director, siggerudk@gao.gov, (202) 512-4400, U.S. Government Accountability Office, 441 G Street NW, Room 7125, Washington, DC 20548
Public Affairs	Chuck Young, Managing Director, youngc1@gao.gov, (202) 512-4800 U.S. Government Accountability Office, 441 G Street NW, Room 7149 Washington, DC 20548